Masterpieces: Artists and Their Works

Matisse

by Ellen Sturm

Consultant:
Joan Lingen, Ph.D.
Professor of Art History
Clarke College
Dubuque, Iowa

Bridgestone Books
an imprint of Capstone Press
Mankato, Minnesota

Bridgestone Books are published by Capstone Press
151 Good Counsel Drive, P.O. Box 669, Mankato, Minnesota 56002.
http://www.capstone-press.com

Library of Congress Cataloging-in-Publication Data
Sturm, Ellen.
 Matisse / by Ellen Sturm.
 p. cm.—(Masterpieces, artists and their works)
 Summary: Discusses the life, works, and lasting influence of Henri Matisse.
 Includes bibliographical references and index.
 ISBN 0-7368-2227-5 (hardcover)
 1. Matisse, Henri, 1869–1954—Juvenile literature. 2. Artists—France—Biography—
Juvenile literature. [1. Matisse, Henri, 1869–1954. 2. Artists. 3. Painting, French.] I. Title.
II. Series.
N6853.M33 S78 2004
709'.2—dc21   2003000065

Editorial Credits
Blake Hoena, editor; Heather Kindseth, series designer; Juliette Peters, book designer;
 Alta Schaffer, photo researcher; Karen Risch, product planning editor

Photo Credits
Art Resource/Scala, cover (left), 14; CNAC/MNAM/Dist. Réunion des Musées
 Nationaux, 8; Réunion des Musées Nationaux, 10 (bottom), 18; The Museum of
 Modern Art/Licensed by Scala, 16, 20
Bridgeman Art Library/Pushkin Museum, Moscow, Russia, 6
Corbis/Bettmann, cover (right); Francis G. Mayer, 4, 10 (top); Archivo Iconografico,
 S.A., 12

1 2 3 4 5 6 08 07 06 05 04 03

Table of Contents

Henri Matisse 5
Young Henri 7
Art Studies 9
Art Styles 11
Fauvism 13
Postimpressionism 15
Moving to the Mediterranean 17
Final Years 19
Matisse's Fame 21

Important Dates 22
Words to Know 23
Read More 23
Useful Addresses 24
Internet Sites 24
Index 24

In *Open Window*, Henri used bright, bold colors instead of lifelike colors. Through the window, boats can be seen floating on pink waves.

Henri Matisse

Henri Matisse (1869–1954) is a famous French artist. He was also a very unusual person. One story says he liked to drive slowly down the middle of the road, blocking traffic. He drove this way so he could enjoy looking at the trees along the street.

Henri is known for working with many art forms. He painted, sculpted, and made etchings. Henri also worked with new art forms. Decoupage is an art form that Henri helped make popular. It involves cutting pieces of colored paper into shapes. Artists then arrange the shapes to make designs.

Henri led the Fauves. This group of artists painted with bright, bold colors. They used colors to show feelings in their art.

Henri believed art did not have to look lifelike. He showed people that art does not have to look real to be beautiful. His ideas changed the way people look at and create art today.

Still lifes are paintings of objects like fruit, vases, and bottles.
Artists paint still lifes to practice using color and shading.
Henri painted the still life *The Bottle of Schiedam* in 1896.

Young Henri

Henri was born December 31, 1869, in Le Cateau, France. While growing up, he did not plan to be an artist. In 1887, he went to law school. A year later, Henri got a job in a law office. He did not think his work was very exciting.

In 1890, Henri became sick with appendicitis. His mother gave him a painting set to keep him busy while he was in the hospital.

At first, Henri copied famous paintings. He then made his own works of art. His first painting was of a river and a mill. For fun, he signed it with his name written backwards, essitaM.

Art excited Henri. He took art classes in the morning before going to work. He also visited museums to see famous works of art.

In 1891, Henri quit his job and moved to Paris, France. He wanted to study at the art schools there. He also wanted to learn from the many well-known artists who lived in Paris.

Woman Reading was one of Henri's first paintings shown at the
Salon. The Salon's judges liked to pick traditional paintings with
lifelike images and dark backgrounds.

Art Studies

Henri began his studies at the Academie Julian. His teachers taught a traditional painting style. This style used dark colors and lifelike images. Henri quickly grew bored with his studies. He wanted to develop his own way of painting.

In 1892, Henri began to study with Gustave Moreau. Moreau was a famous artist who taught at École des Beaux-Arts in Paris. He encouraged Henri to find his own way of painting. He also told Henri to study old paintings. Artists learn how to paint by studying famous works of art.

While studying with Moreau, Henri became a father. In 1894, Caroline Joblaud gave birth to his daughter, Marguerite. Henri and Caroline never married.

In 1896, Henri's studies were rewarded. Some of his paintings were shown at the Salon in Paris. People from around the world came to see and buy art at this gallery. Henri sold two of his paintings.

The Dinner Table (above) was one of Henri's first attempts at Impressionism. People at the Salon did not like this painting because it looked blurry. Girl with Umbrella (right) was painted in the Pointillist style.

Art Styles

In 1897, Henri began to study new art styles. First, he studied Impressionism. Impressionists did not worry about painting lifelike pictures. They wanted to show how something looked at a quick glance. They used broken brush strokes of solid colors. Up close, their paintings look like they are covered with dabs of paint. But from a distance, a picture can clearly be seen.

While studying Impressionism, Henri married Amélie Parayre. She and Henri had two sons, Jean and Pierre. Amélie also helped raise Marguerite.

During this time, Henri did not sell many paintings. Amélie opened a hat shop to support their family. She earned money so Henri could spend his time painting.

In the early 1900s, Henri studied Pointillism. Pointillists used small dots of color to paint. Up close, the dots can be seen clearly in their paintings. From a distance, the dots blend together to form a picture.

Henri painted a green stripe down the woman's face in *The Green Stripe (Madame Matisse)*. The stripe shows a clear line between light and shadow on her face. Henri displayed this Fauvist painting in 1905.

Fauvism

With Impressionism and Pointillism, Henri worked using bright, solid colors. This use of color led Henri to develop his own style of painting. Henri stopped painting objects in lifelike colors. Instead, he used colors to show feelings in his art. Red might show excitement. Orange could show love.

In 1905, Henri displayed his work with other artists who used colors in similar ways. At first, people thought these artists were crazy. People called them "les fauves," or "the wild beasts," because of their wild use of color. Later, people called these artists Fauvists. Many people were interested in their new art style. Henri became rich selling his Fauvist paintings.

Henri continued to change his painting style as he worked. He began to paint objects in simple, flat shapes. He often painted the objects in one solid color. He also stopped using the bright colors of his earlier Fauvist paintings.

Henri used three main colors to paint the people and background in *Music*. He also did not give the people many details. He made this painting simple to create a peaceful scene.

Postimpressionism

In 1908, Henri finished *Harmony in Red* (shown on cover). This painting shows how his style had changed. Henri used bright colors, but objects in the painting did not look real. They looked flat.

Russian art collector Sergeu Shchukin bought *Harmony in Red*. People in Paris called him the "Mad Russian" because he liked new and unusual art. In 1909, Shchukin hired Henri to paint *Dance* and *Music*. Over time, Shchukin bought nearly 40 of Henri's paintings.

In 1910, British art expert Roger Fry held an art exhibit in London, England. Art by Paul Cézanne, Georges Seurat, Paul Gauguin, Vincent van Gogh, and Henri was shown at this exhibit. These artists had different styles. But they all painted objects in colors and shapes that were not lifelike. Fry called them Postimpressionists because these artists had once painted in the Impressionist art style. After Impressionism, they began working with new styles, like Fauvism.

un moment
di libres.
Ne devrait-on
pas faire ac.
complir un
grand voyage
en avion aux
jeunes gens
ayant terminé
leurs études.

54

This page from Henri's book *Jazz* shows a picture called *Icarus*.
Henri made the original picture with colored pieces of paper.

Moving to the Mediterranean

In 1917, Henri moved his family to Nice, France. This city is near the Mediterranean Sea. There, Henri painted scenes of the sea. Some of his works were also of women.

While in Nice, Henri worked on many projects. He made statues like *Seated Nude* and *The Back*. He made 29 drawings called etchings for Stephane Mallarme's book *Poesies*. Henri also made etchings for *Ulysses* by James Joyce. He even made the costumes and set for a ballet called *Rouge de Noir*.

In 1947, Henri published *Jazz*. In this book, Henri wrote about his thoughts on life and art. The book included many brightly colored pictures. Henri said he created these pictures by "drawing with scissors." He cut pieces of paper, painted them in different colors, and arranged them in patterns. This art form became known as decoupage.

Henri designed the altar (center) and stained glass windows (left) for the Chapel of Saint-Marie du Rosaire. He also painted murals on the church's walls.

Final Years

In the early 1940s, Henri had an operation to remove cancer from his stomach. He never fully recovered. For the rest of his life, he spent a great deal of time in bed.

Henri did not let his illness stop him from working. At one point, he tied a piece of chalk to a stick. He used it to draw on the walls and ceiling of his room. Much of Henri's later artwork was made while working in bed.

In 1947, an official from the Chapel of Saint-Marie du Rosaire in Vence, France, visited Henri. He asked Henri to decorate the church. Henri made stained glass windows for the church. He also designed an altar, furniture, and robes for the priests.

On the church's walls, Henri painted several murals. He wanted to keep these paintings simple. He outlined people and objects in black paint. He did not fill the paintings in with many details. Henri hoped the simple pictures would be understood by everyone.

Henri sculpted *La Serpentine* in 1909. Even in his statues, he used few details to show people.

Matisse's Fame

During the last years of his life, Henri was often ill. But he continued to make art. He designed stained glass windows, sculpted, and worked with decoupage until his death. Henri died November 3, 1954. He was 84.

Henri greatly changed people's ideas about art. His work with different art styles taught people that art did not have to be realistic in color. He showed that colors and simple shapes could show meaning.

Henri also helped develop new types of art. Fauvism showed feelings through color. Decoupage is often used today to make decorations.

Henri's art is on display in museums around the world. The Museum of Modern Art in New York shows some of his work. Many of his paintings are at the Pompidou Center in Paris, the Musée Matisse in Nice, and the Pushkin Museum in Moscow, Russia.

Important Dates

1869—Henri is born December 31, in Le Cateau, France.

1887—Henri goes to law school.

1891—Henri quits his job and moves to Paris, France, to study art.

1892—Henri meets Gustave Moreau.

1894—Henri's daughter, Marguerite, is born.

1896—The Salon displays several of Henri's paintings.

1899—Henri's son Jean is born

1900—Henri's son Pierre is born.

1905—The Fauvist art movement begins.

1910—Henri shows his work with the Postimpressionists.

1914—World War I begins; the war ends in 1918.

1917—Henri and his family move to Nice, France.

1939—World War II begins; the war ends in 1945.

1947—Henri publishes *Jazz*, a book about his thoughts on art and life.

1951—Henri finishes the stained glass windows, murals, and furniture for the Chapel of Saint-Marie du Rosaire.

1954—Henri dies of a heart attack on November 3.

Words to Know

altar (AWL-tur)—a large table used for religious ceremonies
appendicitis (uh-pen-duh-SYE-tuhss)—a disease of the appendix; the appendix is a small, closed tube attached to the large intestine.
decoupage (day-koo-PAHZH)—the art of decorating with colored cutouts of paper
etching (ECH-ing)—a picture created on a metal plate; an artist uses an etching to make prints of a picture.
Fauvism (FOH-vi-zuhm)—an art movement using bright, bold colors to show feelings
gallery (GAL-uh-ree)—a place where art is shown and sold
Impressionism (im-PREH-shuh-ni-zuhm)—an art style in which artists painted in broken brush strokes
mural (MYU-ruhl)—a large painting on a wall or a ceiling

Read More

Flux, Paul. *Henri Matisse.* The Life and Work Of. Chicago: Heinemann Library, 2002.
O'Connor, Jane. *Henri Matisse: Drawing with Scissors.* Smart About Art. New York: Grosset & Dunlap, 2002.

Useful Addresses

Baltimore Museum of Art
10 Art Museum Drive
Baltimore, MD 21218-3898

Museum of Modern Art
11 West 53rd Street
New York, NY 10019

Internet Sites

Do you want to find out more about Matisse?
Let FactHound, our fact-finding hound dog,
do the research for you.

Here's how:
1) Visit *http://www.facthound.com*.
2) Type in the **BOOK ID** number: **0736822275**.
3) Click on **FETCH IT**.

FactHound will fetch Internet sites picked by our editors just for you!

Index

decoupage, 5, 17, 21
etchings, 5, 17
Fauvism, 5, 12, 13, 15, 21
Impressionism, 10, 11, 13, 15
Jazz, 16, 17
Moreau, Gustave, 9

museums, 7, 21
Pointillism, 10, 11, 13
Salon, 8, 9, 10
shapes, 5, 13, 15, 21
stained glass windows, 18,
   19, 21